CW00487270

POLPERRO REFLECTIONS

BOSSINEY BOOKS

1

Published in 1994 by Bossiney Books, St Teath, Bodmin, Cornwall.

Typeset and printed by Penwell Ltd, Callington, Cornwall

ISBN 0 948158 94 8

ACKNOWLEDGEMENTS
Front cover photography: ROY WESTLAKE
Front cover design: MAGGIE GINGER
Back cover: CORNISH STUDIES LIBRARY, Redruth
Modern photography: RAY BISHOP, VERN OXLEY,
and A G BARTLETT

Author's Acknowledgements

I AM indebted to Peter and Bridget Bishop of the The Pottery Shop, Polperro for commissioning this second publication on the village and for all their help and encouragement. My special thanks also to local people who have given me interviews and loaned photographs. Mary Richards, the editor of the *Cornish Times*, has generously allowed me to use information concerning the 1993 floods which first appeared in her newspaper, and helped in tracking down photographs of the disaster. Press photographer Vern Oxley of Couch's Great House Restaurant, Polperro, has provided three dramatic shots of the flooding.

Terry Knight and his colleagues of the Cornish Studies Library at Redruth have allowed me into their Cornish Aladdin's Cave: allowing me access to old books about the village – and the use of some rare photographs: 101 thanks.

Last but not least, thanks to Sally Dodd for her typing and valuable contacts, and to Angela Larcombe for her perceptive editing.

2

About the Author . . .

*MICHAEL WILLIAMS, a Cornishman, is the author of **About Polperro**, published in the spring of 1992. Now he completes a south coast double with **Polperro Reflections**. His recent contributions to the Bossiney list include **Psychic Phenomena of the West** and, as co-author, **King Arthur in the West**. He and his wife Sonia live in a cottage on the shoulder of a green valley just outside St Teath in North Cornwall.*

In addition to writing and publishing Michael Williams is a keen cricketer and collector of cricket memorabilia. He was the first captain of the Cornish Crusaders Cricket Club and is today President of the Crusaders. He is also a member of Cornwall and Gloucestershire County Cricket Clubs.

A member of the the International League for the Protection of Horses and the RSPCA, he has worked hard for reform in laws relating to animal welfare. In 1984 he was elected to The Ghost Club and is convinced Cornwall is the most haunted area in the British Isles.

3

Polperro Reflections

THERE is nothing quite like Polperro in all Cornwall. It is unique.

The older parts of Polperro – the heart of the place – conjure up images of a vanished way of Cornish life. The narrow winding streets, over-hung, here and there, by oddly built houses, the sight and scent of the sea, the memory of smugglers and press gangs, the cries of the gulls, the changing faces of sky and water, the rich history and folklore of Polperro and its coastline and countryside, all combine to make it special.

Cliffs to the west and to the east, rising something like four hundred feet, suddenly stop at the entrance to the harbour, and houses cling to the sloping sides of the land with the tenacity of hill goats.

Somebody has said 'These houses tumble about each other's ears ...' This village oozes character and individuality. You could not mistake Polperro for a Devon or *any* English village by the sea.

The inland roads from Looe or Fowey strike the Polperro Valley at Crumplehorn, but a wise perceptive walker once told me the best way to approach the village is along the coastal path through Talland from Looe. He rated it a 'great Cornish experience'.

The whole area has a strong visual quality. Maybe that is why it has attracted so many painters. But I am inclined to think the reason is more subtle: a combination of light and colour, a mixture of material and the magical perhaps. There is *some* indefinable lure.

When you come to, say Mevagissey and Polperro on the south coast, and Padstow and St Ives on the north, you begin to understand how the development of our harbours – the skill of native ship and boat builders and the audacity of our Cornish mariners – have been vital factors in the making of Cornwall and Cornish history.

S P B Mais, when he came here in the late 1920s, spoke of the angles of the topsy-turvy houses, 'the colours of the blue sea, and the darker blue slate rocks'. He also spoke of 'movement' and movement remains today in the shape of boats and fishermen and birds, especially the gulls. Naturally, if Mr Mais came back tomorrow he would see tremendous changes, but the unexpected angles, the outside staircases, the arched rooms with tiny windows: they all remain.

Travel writers have produced some purple prose about this corner of Cornwall.

Everywhere in Polperro there are steps – many leading to intriguing half-hidden doors. Here is a picture taken in 1914. Many of Cornwall's men went off to fight leaving behind them timeless scenes of working life such as this – the bucket on the wall, the tangle of lines hooked outside the windows.

'Polperro will give you freedom from your worries and a sense of tranquility, for you can sit and dream away long hours, with cries of sea birds, the creak of oar, the leisurely preparations of fishermen in the tiny harbour, as the only sounds likely to disturb the even flow of thoughts that come upon you with refreshing regularity. I think one's first glimpse of Polperro should be from the sea, for it is then that you view, tucked away between grim rocks, the miniature harbour in which lies a tiny fishing fleet. And as you glide into this harbour you see, from the very water's edge, tier upon tier of white-washed cottages, crazily perched, so it seems in haphazard confusion, on inaccessible ledges, while rising above this singular sight are green hills and trees wonderful to behold.'

That was Elvira Herbert writing in the June number of *The Great Highway*, published back in 1927. A year earlier, Ray Alexander in the *Traveller and Clubman* said: *'Those visiting the Cornish Riviera should certainly not fail to visit Polperro ...'* and the *Western Morning News* around that time reflected: *'A perfect nest of tradition and a haven of romance, wedged among impassable hills, sleeping on while the world goes round.'*

Those words, of course, were written before tourism had become a major Cornish industry.

Today, at the height of the holiday season, Polperro is a busy spot – and rightly so because tourism has taken the place of traditional industries like mining, fishing and farming. Mining has all but gone from the Cornish landscape, and farming and fishing need fewer hands nowadays.

Naturally if you can choose your spot in the calendar, then you would do well to avoid the congested periods of late July and August. In Cornwall we cannot boast a settled climate, but we do get some beautiful days and the fact our tourist season has stretched in the last quarter of a century is partly confirmation of the fine weather we often get in spring and autumn. The bonus of early and late holidays for visitors is they then avoid congestion on both beaches and roads.

What is the magnetism of the place? I put that question to a number of visitors. Here are some of their replies.

'Polperro is so different ... it has something special.'

'I've been coming for years but never tire of the village or the people.'

'It's a lovely spot, and an ideal base for touring around other parts. You're within easy reach of Looe, Fowey, Liskeard and even the eastern

Swans in Polperro's harbour – a picture captured on film by Ray Bishop in the autumn of 1993.

More steps – and a donkey waiting patiently below.

side of Bodmin Moor.'
'I feel better for being here ...'
Said Thomas Burke of Tintagel: 'What it has to give must be received individually ...' Mr Burke could have been talking of Polperro. Out of season, I enjoy it most. Then the spirit of the past is strongest, and Polperro, for me anyway, has an energising quality. In some moods, Polperro is a *feeling* as much as a place.

I remember on one visit to the village, probably a quarter of a century

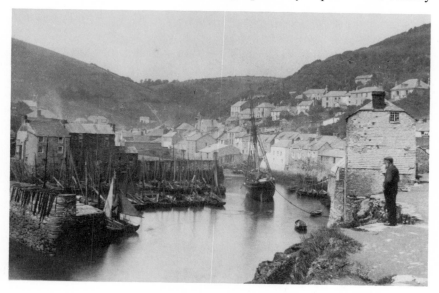

Shrewd editors and publishers know a good picture is worth a thousand words. Here is Polperro photographed around the turn of the century. The camera – or more accurately the man or woman holding the camera – can do a wide range of things: record or probe, identify or analyse. Memory and the camera are very different. Our memory or memories can be highly selective. Some of these early photographers, like this one at Polperro more than ninety years ago, were camera artists. He has truly caught a Polperro reflection. These were the days when the pilchard, not tourism, was the central key to the local economy. Yet even in those times much depended on the weather: a fishing boat confined to harbour because of rough conditions at sea meant loss of money.

ago, coming across some old fishermen talking together and looking out to sea – in memory I can still hear the poetry and the softness of their voices, and talk of choirs, visitors, fishing and too many cars.

As a member of the Ghost Club and someone who has been investigating supernatural cases since 1965, I have a special interest in this village. Ghosts have been seen hereabouts – and Parson Doidge from Talland was reputed to 'raise and lay ghosts at will'. But some said he was in league with the smugglers and this reputation was a good alibi!

There is no doubt that the sea, our Cornish coastline and fishing villages do seem to trigger an exceptional amount of paranormal activity. There have been reports of Cornish ghost ships and the cries of shipwrecked sailors. Of course, the fishermen and their wives were often deeply superstitious.

In the old days too, many of the Polperro cottages would have proudly displayed a hanging horseshoe – for good luck. The horseshoe, made of iron, was regarded as an infallible repellent of witches – sometimes called wise women who worked for good purposes: charming warts and generally acting as spiritual healers.

Polperro, a thirteenth century fishing village, lies within the boundaries of two parishes, Talland and Lansallos. Nature virtually invited a fishing village here: this rock-bound gap in a magical stretch of south Cornish coastline, roughly fifteen miles south west of the Tamar with England beyond.

Polperro inevitably stirs our curiosity. It was a wise Greek who said 'I wanted to know, so I went to see.' Come then, let us explore the place, past as well as present because many of these old pictures have a wonderful knack of taking us back in time – and mood.

'Polperro, a promising recruit' reads the caption on this old picture ▶
postcard. It's interesting to speculate how many hundreds of young men from the village served in the Royal Navy over the years. A cleverly posed photograph or a photographer with a sharp eye for a good picture? Today, we can only guess.

Polperro, "A Promising Recruit."

11

Polperro Memories

EDMUND Jolliff is a Cornishman, to be more precise he is a Polperro man.

'The name Jolliff is sometimes spelt in different ways, but we're all the same family. I was born in the village, in a cottage on the quay in 1907: one of ten children, six boys and four girls. There are only two of us left: me and a younger brother in Australia. My father was the local harbour master and my mother a fisherman's daughter, but I was never tempted to be a fisherman ... it just wasn't my kettle of fish. I went out many times as a boy, only for a trip but I learnt my trade as a carpenter and never regretted it. As an apprentice I earned three shillings a week. We worked from 8am to 5pm five days a week, and on the sixth day, the Saturday, we worked till noon. Then after that first year my wages went up to four shillings a week, and went on rising a shilling a year. Apprentices I've trained couldn't believe it.

'But I loved my work, and am still doing a bit ... yes, some of the older people call me "Jolly" and I suppose I live up to my name in that I'm a very contented man, and have led a very contented life. Holidays have never bothered me. In a way every day in Cornwall is a kind of holiday.

'I've lived and worked here in Polperro all my life except for the war years when I went to work over to Looe, doing carpentry with a boat building firm, all part of the war effort.'

We talked at his home Homelee, The Coombes. 'This house was built in 1933,' he told me; 'and I did all the carpentry involved, and have more or less maintained it until only a few years ago.

'Carpentry has been my life. That and rabbiting and singing in the Polperro choir.' Edmund sang in it from 1923 until 1983 – a musical innings of 60 years. 'We've been on radio and television, and I've sung with the choir in London and in Wales. It's called the Polperro Fisherman's Choir, but they let some of us others into it.

'In my young days, of course, you had to make your own entertainment. No television. As a boy I enjoyed rock climbing and hunting about. The older fishermen were quite kindly men and they'd let you go on the boats.'

'What's the secret then of your long and contented life?'

A thoughtful silence.

'Putting heart and soul into your work. That came first. I never let any-
thing come in front of my work and, of course, I've remained very
active. Over the years, with my dogs, I must have walked hundreds and
hundreds of miles around Polperro, specially on the cliff walks. I've
walked back from Bodinnick many, many times. A five or six mile walk
was nothing for me.'

'What about changes you've seen in Polperro in your life time?'

'Oh, I've seen many. More buildings, more houses, more shops and,
most important of all, more visitors. We need the visitors ... and the pop-
ulation of Polperro has changed. We Cornish seem to be getting fewer.
There was a time when I'd walk down the street and know everybody I
passed. Now some times I'll go down to the quay and not see a person I

know. Years ago there would be groups of men chatting in various parts of the village. Television, I suppose, has changed all that. But I wouldn't want to live anywhere else.'

The Methodists and John Wesley

JOHN Wesley, the preacher on horseback, made great impact in Cornwall. He made two visits to Polperro, and his spirit lives on in many Cornish chapels and homes.

Wesley's preaching and sheer presence shattered old ideas and values. He may have upset some of the Cornish parsons in their comfortable livings, but he spoke a language ordinary Cornish people understood. Tough miners and fishermen, many of whom came to scorn, were among the first to fall upon their knees. Tears and hymns, mingling with confession and conversion, all added to the flames of his evangelism. On one of his Cornish expeditions he wrote *'Many of the lions have become lambs ...'*

It was John Wesley who prodded the Cornish conscience on the subject of smuggling. *'A smuggler then,'* he declared, *and in proportion, every seller or buyer of uncustomed goods is a thief of the first order, a highwayman, or a pickpocket of the worst sort.'*

And after Wesley came a whole army of Nonconformist preachers.

Cornwall is littered with chapels, reminders of Wesley's fiery message and its impact. In the high noon of Methodism those draughty chapels rang with Alleluyas. Today congregations have shrunk but the spirit of Wesley still burns. Attend a Harvest Festival or a Chapel Anniversary service in one of the live chapels and you will understand that he is gone but not forgotten or his brother Charles, for the Cornish, like the Welsh, love a good hymn or song. You can hear some fine singing in some pubs – but that, of course, is another story and would not have met with Mr Wesley's approval.

A serene view of the harbour.

Dick Jolliff and Local Methodism

AT this point I had a second conversation with that well-known Polperro character Dick Jolliff who had talked to me about his fishing days for the earlier publication *About Polperro*. This time, we discussed the impact of Methodism on Polperro.

'Oh, Methodism played a big part in the life of Polperro in the old days,' he recalled. 'There was a time when we had three chapels in the village: Wesleyan, United Methodist and Bible Christian, and all three were well attended. Today there is just one chapel. I started as a boy attending the Sunday School services which were held on Sunday afternoons, and, of course, there were morning and evening services for the adults. In those days there was a strong teetotal commitment, and there were close links between Methodism and the fishermen, a number of them were local preachers or taught in the Sunday School.

'John Wesley preached in the green here and I remember some time in the 1940s the President of the Methodist Conference came and preached in the green, the very spot where the great John Wesley had given his sermon all those years ago. Bishop Hunkin, the Bishop of Truro whose father was a Wesleyan, came and took part in the service: a wonderful occasion.'

Dick Jolliff, who started preaching in 1938 and has preached for more than half a century said: 'The old Looe circuit covered a very wide area. We had chapels from Polruan in the west up as far as Lerryn and Couch's Mill and inland near St Pinnock, a chapel called Bethel, and as far east as Sandplace and Looe. There were chapels all over the place. Of course, in those days the sermon was not only an important part of the service ... for many people the sermon could be the high spot of the week ... you had no television.

'We had some grand preachers, men like Isaac Foot, and I remember hearing Dr Donald Soper, now Lord Soper, on one occasion in Liskeard.

'Methodism was very important for the fishermen of Polperro. They kept the Lord's Day. For many, many years no fishing boat went out from Polperro on a Sunday. Looe fishermen went to sea on a Sunday, but no Polperro men ... not until the 1940s anyway.'

The Bridge of Sighs – a photograph taken in 1914.

The Gull

The sweet blossom lifted in the wind,
I followed it floating down to the sea,
Then I gazed to drink the sight,
The harbour full of life and light,
Beauty's finger beckoned busily about me,

No hush there was, no sacred silence,
No village slept this crystal dawn,
I danced down to spy the fleet,
Of fishermen returned to eat,
Nets full that move and shine in early morn,

Here I feel that time does not advance,
And here perhaps the new ways can't belong,
Yet I fly above fresh, wet sand,
Over boats painted by modern hand,
And somewhere hear a snatch of well known song,

I am given this inimitable present,
A world timeless, necessary, thriving,
Dependent on its salty spoil,
As each man for himself will toil,
Here I belong, the gull, dipping, diving.

KG

Kirsty Gardiner is a young writer who lives near Truro. Here is a poem she has written especially for this publication. 'I wrote about a gull,' she says, 'because I feel that every fishing village and trawler and fisherman himself are somehow bonded together by the gull, always hanging over them, all-seeing, all-knowing and generally all-eating!'

A gull wheeling in flight above the village – a drawing from Bossiney artist Felicity Young.

Frederick Cook at work in his studio.

Frederick Cook, RWA

FREDERICK Cook was a painter who fell in love with Polperro.

A distinguished war painter with a special interest in the fire service – he was a fireman during the London Blitz – a number of his war pictures are at the Imperial War Museum.

A real all-rounder, Frederick Cook was called 'a master of gouache.' He worked with great sense of colour and imagination, producing beautiful pictures of harbour scenes and coastal views, especially in and around Polperro, some of them with an almost surrealist quality. As a result of swimming, he painted some fine and delicate underwater studies. Outside and beyond all this, Frederick Cook was a prolific and accomplished book illustrator: work with great attention to detail. 'He hardly ever stopped painting,' his widow told me recently on a visit to the harbourside home at Polperro. 'He simply loved his work.'

Harbour Studio, with its balcony was originally two old and primitive fishermen's dwellings. Here literally at the water's edge, Frederick Cook, for nearly forty years, produced a rich harvest of varied art, oils, watercolours and drawings.

I first met his work at St Ives, down in West Cornwall, where back in the 60s he exhibited regularly. He and his wife were members of the Council of the St Ives' Society of Artists. Anyon Cook was a fine portrait painter and illustrator for books and magazines. She painted portraits of a number of well-known personalities, including the Princess Royal, then aged seven.

Frederick Cook exhibited in London at the Royal Academy – I saw a photograph of him at a black tie Royal Academy dinner when Sir Winston Churchill was the guest speaker. His work was also seen at the Royal Scottish Academy and in Bristol, at the Royal West of England Academy, Plymouth and occasionally Newlyn – newspaper cuttings from those days confirm the quality and popularity of his art. In a sentence he was an outstanding ambassador for Polperro. He enjoyed his work and life in the village where he was generally known as Freddie – and he lives on in his paintings.

Noughts and Crosses Inn, Polperro, still in use today.

21

A modern shot of Polperro by Ray Bishop of Wadebridge. Ray, who is Bossiney's most prolific photographer, says: 'Polperro must be one of the most photographed places in the whole of the United Kingdom. Visually, it's very attractive, particularly the harbour part; but in summer the photographer often has the problem of too many people spoiling the picturesque. Then, in winter, when the visitors have gone, you need to come around the middle of the day because the sun soon goes down behind the sides of the valley. But it is worth the effort. The older parts of Polperro are among some of the most photogenic in all Cornwall.

Conversation among Polperro fishermen on the quay – only one seems interested in the photographer! This postcard was sent to a lady in Eastbourne, Sussex and reads 'Having a glorious time, darling. Been 90 miles today to Looe and Polperro ...' It was posted during the reign of our Queen's grandfather and postage was precisely one penny. Historically it was penny post which brought written contact within the grasp of every family capable of reading and writing. Before then letter writing had been an expensive business – the postage you paid depended on the distance involved and the number of sheets of paper used. As a result letters were a matter for the wealthy members of society or those engaged in commerce.

23

The 1993 Floods

POLPERRO's latest flood disaster came on Thursday December 30 1993, when cars were swept away like toys, bridges badly damaged and dozens of homes and businesses flooded by a seven-feet wall of water. More than an inch of rain in the space of four hours fell on an already saturated Cornwall. During the month of December the Westcountry had had twice its average rainfall.

An elderly man was rescued from the window of a riverside property by firemen using a ladder to straddle the gushing torrent, and Mervyn Kettle, fire brigade chief assistant divisional officer, who bravely went into the river to rescue a dog, had to be dragged to safety by a fellow fireman and villagers.

Edmund Jolliff told me: 'I've now experienced three Polperro floods in my life time and this was the worst of the three. It happened so quickly. I was looking out of the window and within a matter of minutes it had turned into a raging torrent.'

Two people who agreed with Edmund's assessment are Peter and Betty Nelson of Nelson's Restaurant at Saxon Bridge. Speaking to the *Western Morning News* they said: 'The force and power of the flood was much greater than in 1976.' They had seven feet of water in their basement kitchen.

Jack and Kate Owen, on a visit from London, owners of a holiday home by the harbour, saw their £23,000 Rover floating in the Claremont Hotel car park, but Mrs Owen said: 'Polperro is a great village and it is well worth it. This will not stop us coming here.'

Cornish Times photographer Vern Oxley – the man whose pictures of the 1993 flood appear inside these pages – is the owner of Couch's Great House Restaurant. He told the newspaper: 'It was a miracle nobody was seriously injured. It was really quite frightening. Everything happened so quickly and there was a feeling of helplessness as the water came at us from all directions.'

One of the luckiest characters in the whole village was Bob, a blind Labrador. The ten-year-old black dog was carried half-a-mile into the harbour by the rushing waters after he had gone for a swim in the river.

◀ *Firemen make their way past shops in Lansallos Street as the flood water continues to rise.*

Saxon Bridge is wrecked as the River Pol bursts over the top. The man in the middle distance is standing outside Nelson's Restaurant.

But Bob was lucky. Gerald Leck, 42, who was in a dinghy in the harbour, spotted the dog, got to him just as he went under and managed to drag him into the dinghy.

Retired fisherman Dick Jolliff, whom I interviewed earlier about Methodism, told me: 'It was all pretty grim. In the earlier floods, the ground was firm, but this time the ground was like a sponge and, as a result, more mud came down, and that caused enormous problems.'

Among those who managed a narrow escape were Tony and Gill Mildren, owners of the Mill House Hotel. They had to flee their hotel via the flat roof next door as the water reached the first floor ceiling into the harbour. 'The force of the water ripped the door off its hinges and smashed in the windows,' said Mr Mildren. 'Within minutes it was chest high and we just had time to grab the dog and escape.'

There was also a wet wedding anniversary. Mrs Minnie Toms, 84, of Hope Cottage, The Warren, was celebrating her 60th wedding anniversary with husband Tom, 85, and their family when water flooded their home. 'We were all in the kitchen and suddenly the water started com-

ing through the ceiling from the sitting room above,' said Mrs Toms. 'We have had water pouring down the lane ... but this is the first time it has ever come in.'

South East Cornwall MP Robert Hicks, accompanied by his wife Glenys, visited the village on the following Monday, and hit out at 'the inertia' following the 1976 flooding.

Speaking to the *Cornish Times* Mr Hicks said: 'In September 1976 I never envisaged that 17 years later I would be talking to the same people in the same properties and witnessing identical devastation and havoc. On that occasion people felt afterwards it was a one-off phenomenon – something that could only happen once in a generation.

'Clearly that was not the case and it is imperative that an early examination of the factors that led to the current disaster be undertaken by the NRA.'

Robert Hicks went on: 'It is important that the River Pol is recognised as a major stream in order that government grant aid can be made available to the NRA. Secondly we must look to the potential of European funding as the whole community is affected, tourism being the mainstay of the area.'

* * * * *

◀   *Looking down Mill Hill.*

The 1993 floods were far from the first Polperro has had to endure. On Friday September 1976 around 8pm a thunderstorm erupted and within a matter of minutes a nightmare situation developed with torrents of water flooding the narrow streets, terrifying residents and damaging more than a hundred properties. This photograph by A G Bartlett shows flood-damaged items belonging to the late Mr and Mrs Plummer of Melrose Cottage, next to the Old Forge.

Harbour Master – Chris Curtis

HARBOUR Masters are important men along the coastline of Cornwall.

In January 1994 I had a conversation with Chris Curtis. He's been Harbour Master at Polperro since 1982, and comes from an old Polperro family. His father and his grandfather were fishermen.

'Six generations of the family have been fishermen, possibly seven. In 1926 my father was awarded a certificate for his bravery in rescuing the survivor of a wrecked schooner. We're proud of that.'

Chris is a real all-rounder: one of the unpaid trustees who run the harbour – 'The people of Polperro were given their harbour by royal charter in 1894' – he is a working fisherman and does pleasure trips for the visitors in the summer. 'We plan to open a smuggling and fishing museum in part of the old fish factory in 1994.'

Chris Curtis is also a painter. 'I work in oils and water colours, mainly scenes of old Polperro and fishing. These are the subjects that excite me as a painter.'

In its heyday, as many as fifty to sixty fishing boats went out from the village. 'Today only nine boats go out from Polperro,' he said – you could hear the sigh in his Cornish voice – 'fishing's declining all the time. It's very sad. Little prospect for the next generation and young men have to move away from the village to find work. I sit on a lot of fishing committees and it's comparatively rare that you hear a Cornish voice. And it's not just fishing. More and more upcountry people are coming into Cornwall. I've nothing against them personally as individuals ... but there just isn't the same identity and commitment. It weakens the spirit of the community.'

But Cornwall and Polperro in particular are fortunate to have men the calibre of Chris Curtis. His whole life personifies that independence and *Cornishness* which makes Cornwall a people and a place apart.

Finally we talked about the latest flooding.

'The tide being out helped the overall situation considerably. The harbour gate was closed but there was so much debris against that gate that the water rose to fourteen feet inside the harbour. But I dared not open the gate. The volume of water would have been dam bursting and boats would have been swept out to sea.'

30

Above, harbour master Chris Curtis and, below, a scene from earlier days as fishermen sold their catch on the harbour front.

Ye Olde Porch, Polperro.

▲

A quiet day in Polperro Harbour many years ago. Inland dwellers may be inclined to take our Cornish ports and harbours for granted. But when we come to places like Polperro we are reminded of our vast maritime tradition. Harbours cannot be mass-produced. Each one has a character of its own. Leo Walmsley, in his book **British Ports & Harbours**, published by Collins in 1942, wrote: **'The real beauty of the original Cornish fishing village with its white-washed cottages, slate roofs and winding streets, is not the quaintness of them, but that they were built honestly by simple and honest people out of native material without any pretensions to "art".'** *And with the Hitler War raging he reflected: '... the least spoilt and loveliest of them all is Polperro ...'*

◀ *An errand man with a basket waits at the top of the hill as a trap pulled by a donkey plods upwards on its way. A peaceful scene from less complicated days with deserted streets and an uninterrupted view to the fields above the village.*

Couch's House

COUCH'S House must be one of the most photographed buildings in this corner of Cornwall. Here it is as two drawings on an old picture postcard. Dr Jonathan Couch, the man they called 'the old doctor', married three times. His first wife died in childbirth, and his second wife Jane Quiller inherited the property when her mother died and to this day it is known as Couch's House. At the age of 70, Jonathan Couch sprung a surprise by marrying Sarah Lander Roose who was forty eight years his junior.

In addition to being a busy doctor for the area, Jonathan Couch made valuable contributions to natural history. Like Dr William Borlase down in West Cornwall, he remained loyal to Cornwall and her people. Both men had gifts that might have taken them far away from Cornwall and earned them a good deal more money. Pope once wrote of Borlase 'In the shade, but shining,' and the same could be said of Dr Couch here at Polperro.

No. 46   COUCH'S HOUSE — POLPERRO.

COUCH'S HOUSE, POLPERRO.

MERVYN CHAMBERS

Dr Jonathan Couch: a magnificent character photograph of Polperro's most distinguished son, loaned for this publication by the Cornish Studies Library at Redruth. Jonathan Couch produced a vast amount of published and sadly unpublished work. His greatest published achievement was his **History of the Fishes of the British Isles** *which he started writing in 1862 and completed three years later in four volumes. Polperro fishermen helped him in his work by bringing specimens fresh from the sea to his door.*

Cecil Williamson who ran the smuggling museum at Polperro for many
years. He also has a witchcraft museum at Boscastle. Personally I have
only been interested in white witches – those who operate for good purposes. Mr Williamson told me 'The simple fact of life is that all magic
making depends upon the help and participation of a spirit force. A force
which, as a thought form is silent, and yet has the pulse of life. How to
establish a union and understanding with this supernatural force is the
secret of your Cornish Aunty May. Why Aunty May? Well, with the true
Celtic nimble wit of the Cornish, the answer is "Maybe she will help
you and maybe not!" So going to see Aunty Maybe got shortened to "Go
and see Aunty May."

CORNISH LITANY.

From Ghoulies & Ghosties
And long-leggetty beasties
And things that go bump
in the night
Good Lord, deliver us!

PUBLISHED BY THE POLPERRO PRESS AT 'THE HOUSE ON THE PROPS'.

38

A Cornish Litany

THIS picture postcard contains a splendid Cornish litany in respect of matters supernatural.

I sometimes wonder *why* there should be so much psychic phenomena in Cornwall and in small communities like Polperro. Our Celtic ancestry comes into this, I'm sure, but we must not forget that the wives of fishermen and miners could turn into widows through a boat lost at sea or a disaster down a mine. Consequently signs and omens assumed a special significance.

In Cornwall, particularly along the coast, people sound in body and mind, have experienced 'time slips', occasions when they have found themselves in the past. Not for nothing did Professor C.E.M. Joad of BBC Radio 'Brains Trust' fame once refer to 'the undoubted queerness of time.'

I have a theory that the thing we call time is like a film and it may get tangled or twisted and, as a result, we pick up fragments of other times – and other people.

Smuggling

THE SHEER geography made Polperro a perfect rendezvous for smugglers – that and the co-operation of local people! It is the habit of many writers to portray smugglers in a flattering romantic way. Often they are seen as rich young men more interested in adventure than law breaking and sometimes as double agents in the conflicts between these islands and France. In reality many of them were violent characters, capable of treachery and even murder.

Smuggling was a curiously grey area of operation. During the two-hundred-year-long battle between the Revenue men and the Cornish smugglers, there was a kind of mutual respect but there were no real 'laws of the game.'

David Mudd in his *Around & About the Smugglers' Ways* recalled what might have happened in a Polperro inn one evening:

'If the door burst open and someone dashed in to cry 'e's dead', conversation would stop to await further details of whether the victim was an Excise officer or a smuggler. Reactions would be contradictory. Far from greeting the news of an officer's death, many smugglers would be inclined towards sadness out of genuine regret at the loss of life. Others, although tempted to rejoice, would be fearful as to the extra activity in the community as every possible step would be taken to trace the culprits. Similarly, the law officers would regard the death of a smuggler with a mixture of caution and relief. Were he a known man of violence, then the world were well rid of him. If, however, he were the victim of excessive zeal and incompetence, the community would unite against the forces of Customs and Excise and even informers would remain silent.'

Yes, a curious, grey world. Boats sailed out of Cornish harbours. Were they on a legal journey? Would they bring back fish or brandy and tobacco? Questions hovered, and there were sometimes whispered allegations about ministers of the church and magistrates: men normally regarded as respectable pillars of Cornish society.

Even in the last years of this, the twentieth century, the older parts of ▶ *the village stir our curiosity. In the eye of our imagination we can picture the place when it was peopled by smugglers.*

Polperro, A Street Scene.

This quaint couple are studying a holiday poster on an old Cornish railway station. The coming of the railway, of course, changed the face of Cornwall in that it brought the holiday-makers and sowed the seeds of expanding tourism. The trains never came here to Polperro. Looe was – and remains – the nearest railway station. Through tourism though the character and personality of the Polperro district began to change: the cottagers offering bed and breakfast, the farmers' wives providing Cornish teas, and the local fishermen rowing the visitors out from the coast to catch the fish they would have otherwise caught for themselves.

Today tourism is a major plank in the Cornish economy. The Cornish air continues to invigorate and the contrast and variety of our Cornish coastline and countryside remain powerful magnets. ▶

◀

*Polperro, a street scene: This lovely old picture postcard sometimes appears minus the old fishwife seen on the left which prompts this question 'Did she suddenly appear and the photographer decide to include her?' My earlier **About Polperro** contains the card minus the lady. The passion for collecting picture postcards – like so many other things – began in Victorian times, and the Queen herself was a collector. It is remarkable to think that in those more leisurely days you could send a card late in the afternoon announcing your arrival at a certain destination on a certain train the very next day, knowing the card would arrive first. Many who met friends or relations at Liskeard or Looe station would have been informed in this way. Our Edwardian ancestors though would be astonished to discover that cards they bought for a penny have gone up two hundred per cent in value! Such cards have become collectors' items. The fact is about only ten cards in a hundred have survived. Our grandparents either burnt them or put them in the dustbin.*

43

Jan and Jane's Holiday.

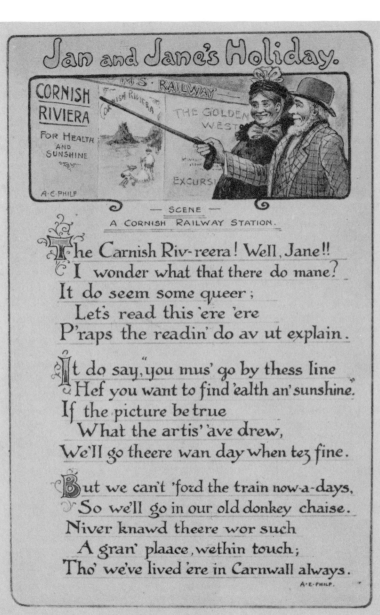

— SCENE —
A CORNISH RAILWAY STATION.

The Carnish Riv-reera! Well, Jane!!
  I wonder what that there do mane?
It do seem some queer;
   Let's read this 'ere 'ere
P'raps the readin' do av ut explain.

It do say, "you mus' go by thess line
  Hef you want to find 'ealth an' sunshine."
If the picture be true
   What the artis' 'ave drew,
We'll go theere wan day when tez fine.

But we can't 'ford the train now-a-days,
  So we'll go in our old donkey chaise.
Niver knawd theere wor such
   A gran' plaace, wethin touch;
Tho' we've lived 'ere in Carnwall always.

A·E·PHILP.

44

The Cornish Pasty

THE CORNISH pasty can be a feast – a moveable feast at that. Sadly though no food has been so run down, so badly imitated.

Historically, the first pasties were cooked in the late 1700s for the lower orders. The march of time and good sense in Cornish kitchens, however, combined to improve the quality, and in its heyday the pasty was a complete meal: meat and vegetables at one end, and apples and clotted cream at the other.

Miners in particular valued the Cornish pasty; though for some strange superstitious reason Cornish fishermen were loth to take a pasty to sea – or saffron cake for that matter. In the mines, there was a strange little tradition in the old days, in that a miner was always supposed to leave a 'corner' of his pasty for the 'knockers', as the evil spirits were called. it must have been a terrible temptation because many of us think the 'corner' is the best bit.

Some Cornish folk insist the Devil has never crossed the Tamar for fear of being put into a Cornish pasty, but one story goes that Old Nick did, in fact, come into Cornwall. He descended on a fishing village, and

CORNISH PASTY AND A DISH O' TAY

45

The old bake-oven at Polperro. It would have been heated with faggots of wood and produced not only bread, rolls and perhaps saffron buns for sale but served as an oven for those cottagers without baking facilities who would have brought along meat, pies and puddings to collect later.

peering through the door of a cottage he saw a housewife making a conger eel pie. Old Nick was curious and enquired about the contents of the pie. The housewife, summing him up shrewdly, replied: 'You must be the Devil they talk about ... if you don't depart quickly, I'll put you into the pie!'

I like to think such an encounter took place here at Polperro.

Polperro Postscript

WHY is Polperro such a special place for so many people? There is perhaps no single crystal-clear explanation – visitors and locals I have spoken to have given good but different reasons.

I remember the Cornish painter Margo Maeckelberghe once saying to me 'The most important part, for me, is this mysterious X an artist must *feel* about a place to paint it.'

Conceivably *that* indefinable something makes Polperro such an interesting location.

'X' marks the spot. It's fascinating to reflect this fact: thousands of visitors have marked their postcards from the village with X – marking where they stayed or where they had a meal, quite material down-to-earth reasons. Yet the X factors hovers over the village.

In 1993 Ray Bishop and I came here to do some photography; Eva Routland, a young Cornish girl, who hopes to become a model, came with us, her first visit to Polperro. It was a dreadful day in terms of weather – the forecasters had got it completely wrong. But on the homeward journey Eva told us she had enjoyed her visit and thought Polperro 'a lovely place.' Maybe that tells us a lot about the village and the people here. Her young words might even go to the heart of the matter.

MORE BOSSINEY BOOKS . . .

ABOUT POLPERRO
by Michael Williams

EAST CORNWALL IN THE OLD DAYS
by Joy Wilson

THE CRUEL CORNISH SEA
by David Mudd
David Mudd selects more than 30 Cornish shipwrecks, spanning 400 years, in his fascinating account of seas and a coastline that each year claim their toll of human lives.
'This is an important book.' **Lord St. Levan, Cornish Times**

GHOSTS OF CORNWALL
by Peter Underwood, the man rated Britain's no 1 ghost hunter.

DAPHNE du MAURIER COUNTRY
by Martyn Shallcross
'A treasure chest for those who love Cornwall and the du Maurier novels.'
Valerie Mitchell, The Packet Newspapers

DISCOVERING BODMIN MOOR
by E V Thompson

SECRET CORNWALL
Introduced by Madeleine Gould of BBC Radio Cornwall

SUPERNATURAL INVESTIGATION
by Michael Williams
'... has to be the one you read in front of a roaring fire, curtains closed against the howling gale and a stiff whisky within arm's reach to calm the nerves.'
Wendy Hanwell, Tavistock Times

MYSTERIES OF THE SOUTH WEST
by Tamsin Thomas of BBC Radio Cornwall
A tour of ancient sites in Cornwall and on Dartmoor.

SUPERNATURAL SEARCH IN CORNWALL
by Michael Williams
Investigates various facets of the paranormal in Cornwall.
'Fascinating reading.' **Nancy Hammonds, Evening Herald.**

We shall be pleased to send you our catalogue giving full details of our growing list of titles for Cornwall, Devon, Dorset, Somerset, Avon and Wiltshire. If you have difficulty in obtaining our titles, write direct to Bossiney Books, Land's End, St Teath, Bodmin, Cornwall.